SEP 2009

Salamanders

And Other Animals With Amazing Tails

by
Susan Labella

Children's Press®
A Division of Scholastic Inc.
New York Toronto London Auckland Sydney
Mexico City New Delhi Hong Kong
Danbury, Connecticut

These content vocabulary word builders
are for grades 1-2.

Consultant: Dr. Dale Madison
Department of Biological Sciences
Binghamton University
Binghamton, New York

Reading Specialist: Don Curry
Curriculum Specialist: Linda Bullock

Special thanks to Omaha's Henry Doorly Zoo

Photo Credits:

Photographs © 2005: Animals Animals/Breck P. Kent: 7; Corbis Images: 5 bottom right, 19 (Amos Nachoum); Dembinsky Photo Assoc.: cover background (Gary Meszaros), 5 bottom left, 15 (Skip Moody); Dwight R. Kuhn Photography: cover center inset, back cover, 4 top, 5 top right, 9, 10, 11; Nature Picture Library Ltd.: 23 bottom right (Jeff Foott), 4 bottom right, 13 (Tony Heald), 3, 22 (Barry Mansell), 23 top right (Anup Shah); NHPA: cover left inset, 5 top left, 17 (Mark Bowler); Peter Arnold Inc.: 23 top left (S. J. Krasemann), 20, 21 (R. Andrew Odum); Photo Researchers, NY: 2 (Suzanne L. & Joseph T. Collins), 1 (Dante Fenolio), 12 (Jeff Lepore); PhotoEdit: 4 bottom left, 8 (Susan Van Etten); Seapics.com: 23 bottom left (Rudie Kuiter), cover right inset (Ingrid Visser).

Book Design: Simonsays Design!

Library of Congress Cataloging-in-Publication Data

Labella, Susan, 1948-
    Salamanders and other animals with amazing tails / by Susan Labella.
        p. cm.–(Scholastic news nonfiction readers)
    Includes bibliographical references and index.
    ISBN 0-516-24929-0 (lib. bdg.)   0-516-24780-8 (pbk.)
    1. Tail–Juvenile literature. I. Title. II. Series.
    QL950.6.L33 2005
    590–dc22

                                                        2005002088

1 2 3 4 5 6 7 8 9 10 R 14 13 12 11 10 09 08 07 06 05

CONTENTS

WORD HUNT

Look for these words as you read. They will be in **bold**.

gecko
(**geck**-oh)

predator
(**pred**-uh-tur)

quills
(kwils)

howler monkey
(**how**-ler **muhng**-kee)

poisonous tail
(**poi**-zuh-nuhs tale)

squirrel
(skwurl)

tail flukes
(tale flooks)

5

Tails! Tails!

How does an animal use its tail?

An animal can use its tail to hurt or trick animals that want to eat it.

It can use its tail to move in trees or swim in water, too.

Let's look at some animals that have amazing tails!

This is a mud puppy salamander.
Its tail helps it swim.

Spotted salamanders have **poisonous tails**.

The poison can hurt a **predator**.

A garter snake is a predator. It eats salamanders.

garter snake

This is a spotted salamander.
Its tail has poison in it.

A **gecko** uses its tail to trick a predator.

If an animal bites the gecko's tail, the tail breaks off.

The gecko gets away. Later, it grows another tail.

tail growing

This is a gecko.
Its tail is gone!

After a few months, its
tail starts to grow back.

How does a porcupine scare away animals that want to eat it?

It uses its **quills**!

Quills are sharp hairs that cover a porcupine's tail.

It can push its quills into another animal. Ouch!

quills

The quills on this porcupine are sharp!

A **squirrel** uses its tail to balance on tree branches.

That means its tail keeps it from falling over.

Will this squirrel fall? No. Its tail is helping it balance.

A **howler monkey** has a strong tail.

It uses its tail to help it swing from branch to branch.

tail

A whale uses its **tail flukes** to swim fast. It swims fast to catch prey, or animals to eat.

These fish are prey.

This killer whale uses its strong tail flukes to chase the fish.

Chomp! There are lots of fish to eat.

fish

tail flukes

A GECKO'S TAIL

1 Look! This gecko lost its tail. It was attacked by a predator.

2 In 7 days, a new tail begins to grow. The tail is a different color.

GROWS BACK!

5 This gecko tricked its predator, and now it has a new tail!

4 Wow! After 2 months, the tail is fully-grown.

3 The tail grows and grows. It gets longer and changes color.

21

YOUR NEW WORDS

gecko (**geck**-oh) a small lizard with padded toes that lives in warm places

howler monkey (**how**-ler **muhng**-kee) a monkey that lives in Central or South America

poisonous tail (**poi**-zuh-nuhs tale) a tail that is bad to eat

predator (**pred**-uh–tur) an animal that hunts other animals for food

quills (kwils) a porcupine has sharp, stiff hairs called quills

squirrel (skwurl) a rodent that climbs trees and has a bushy tail

tail flukes (tale flooks) parts of a whale's tail

THESE ANIMALS HAVE AMAZING TAILS, TOO!

deer

elephant

rattlesnake

sea horse

INDEX

FIND OUT MORE

Book:
What Do You Do with a Tail Like This?
by Robin Page and Steve Jenkins

Website:
Wildmagazine.ca
http://www.wildinfo.com

MEET THE AUTHOR:

Susan Labella is a freelance writer of books, articles, and magazines for kids. She is the author of other books in the *Scholastic News Nonfiction Readers* series. She lives in rural Connecticut where she sees squirrels with bushy tails in her backyard.